ISBN-13: 978-1546452829

ISBN-10: 1546452826

Illustrations by Kristen Rabideau at www.drawn2bcreative.com

Clip art used with permission, and created by Natalie Clevenger and The ClipArt Factory at www.teacherspayteachers.com/Store/The-Clipart-Factory

Book Design by Jennifer Sharpe

Published by Jennifer Sharpe
sharpefamily0824@sbcglobal.net

# THE
# MASS BOOK
## for Catholic
## Children

This book belongs to:

_____

# BY: Jennifer Sharpe

# A NOTE FOR PARENTS

Dear Parents,

You've purchased this book for your child because you know that the Mass is something special--something you want your children to cherish as much as you do. It's right and good that you want to share the joy of the Mass with your children, and it is my hope that this book will help you do that.

You may find that as your child works through the different activities laid out in this book, they come to you with questions. Some you will be able to answer; some you may not be able to answer. And that's okay. Don't be afraid to tell your child that you don't know everything there is to know about the Mass, or about Jesus, or about Sacred Scripture. Instead, learn together. It may be that the more you are willing to learn with them, the more curious your child will grow about their faith. And that's a good thing!

So, if after using this book for a while your child comes to you with a question you can't readily answer, don't panic! Open your Bible or a catechism with them, or make a visit to the Catholic bookstore for some new reading material. You are your child's first teacher of the faith, and God will equip you for the task.

May this book be a blessing to your family, and awaken in your child a deep love for the Mass.

In Christ,

Jennifer Sharpe

# HOW TO USE THIS BOOK

Do you go to Mass on Sundays and Holy Days? If someone has purchased this book for you, I'll bet that you do. And I'll bet that you are pretty familiar with the parts of the Mass already. But do you ever have trouble focusing your mind on what is happening during Mass? Do you ever leave Mass and forget what the readings were about? Or maybe you love Jesus, but struggle to pray to him during Mass. *The Mass Book for Catholic Children* is designed to help you participate in the Mass to the fullest. For each Mass, there are nine different activities for you to complete. These activities begin when you wake up in the morning to get ready for Mass, and they don't stop until Mass has ended!

In the following pages, I am going to walk you through how each activity works, giving you suggestions and helpful tips on how you can make the most of the Mass. After all, the Mass is one of God's most precious gifts to us. In it, we get to meet Jesus--in the Holy Gospel, in the people around us, and most especially in the Blessed Sacrament.

For each Mass you will be given three pages to complete. Feel free to complete as much or as little as you like. This book is here to help you engage in the Mass. It is not just a busy book or something to keep you quiet during Mass, but a worship aide. So if you find that you get too distracted by some of the activities, skip them! But be sure to do the ones that *do* help you to focus. Look through the next three pages to see exactly how each activity works!

## Am I Ready to Meet Jesus in the Mass?

# A CHECKLIST

You know, every time we go to Mass, we have a chance to meet Jesus; he is there in the readings from Sacred Scripture, he is there in the hearts of the people around us, and in a very special way he is truly present to give himself to us in the Eucharist. So it's best to get prepared beforehand, don't you think? Go ahead and read through the checklist in this box and make a little check by each item that you have completed. Challenge yourself! Can you check off all six items?

## Liturgical Color

Color the priest's vestments the correct liturgical color. This can help you remember what season we are in. You can color it during Mass, or just make note of the color and do it later.

Make a tally mark each time you hear the words:

## "Jesus Christ"

You'll be surprised how many times these words are said during Mass, but it is no wonder, since they are the most important words you will ever hear. Each time you make a mark, send up a silent prayer thanking Jesus for meeting you at Mass today!

## Responsorial Psalm

Write the little phrase that you sing as part of the Psalm here. Have you ever noticed those little phrases before? They make wonderful short prayers! Later you can pray those words when you are having a tough time, or just can't think of what to pray.

## Gospel Story

Write the name of the gospel story here. That way you won't forget what the reading was about that day!

Go ahead and draw a picture of the gospel story here. Sometimes seeing the story in a picture really helps us remember it. And later in the week, you can go back and look at your picture as you pray, thanking Jesus for the wonderful things he did during his life on earth.

## Draw the Gospel Story

# Words to Listen For During Mass
## Circle each word you hear.

Your mind may wander sometimes. It's okay. Jesus understands that. But use this list to help you focus during the homily. Keep your listening ears on, and whenever you hear a word from the list, circle it. See how many you can hear!

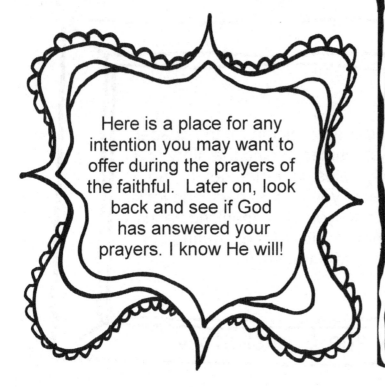

Here is a place for any intention you may want to offer during the prayers of the faithful. Later on, look back and see if God has answered your prayers. I know He will!

## Go Forth!
Have you ever noticed these words at the end of Mass? When we go to Mass, we receive grace that allows us to go out into the world, and be kind and merciful to others. Check off each thing you have completed after Mass is over. But most of all try to be extra kind to those around you today!

# Am I Ready to Meet Jesus in the Mass?

## A CHECKLIST

☐ Morning Offering

☐ Had a good attitude when getting ready

☐ Fasted for 1 hour

☐ Arrived on Time

☐ Blessed myself with Holy Water

☐ Prayed before Mass Began

Liturgical Color

Make a tally mark each time you hear the words:
"Jesus Christ"

Responsorial Psalm

Gospel Story

Draw the Gospel Story

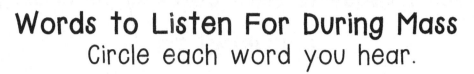

# Words to Listen For During Mass
## Circle each word you hear.

| | | |
|---|---|---|
| Apostles | Grace | Saint |
| Blessed Mother | Holy Spirit | Scripture |
| Communion | Mercy | Sin |
| Eucharist | Prayer | Trinity |
| Faith | Reconciliation | Trust |
| Forgiveness | Sacrament | Virtue |

Lord,
hear my prayer!

_____

_____

_____

## Go Forth!

☐ Received Communion devoutly

☐ Genuflected when I left the pew

☐ Blessed myself with Holy Water when I left

☐ Showed mercy to someone today

# Am I Ready to Meet Jesus in the Mass?

## A CHECKLIST

☐ Morning Offering

☐ Had a good attitude when getting ready

☐ Fasted for 1 hour

☐ Arrived on Time

☐ Blessed myself with Holy Water

☐ Prayed before Mass Began

Liturgical Color

Make a tally mark each time you hear the words:
**"Jesus Christ"**

Responsorial Psalm

Gospel Story

Draw the Gospel Story

# Words to Listen For During Mass
## Circle each word you hear.

| | | |
|---|---|---|
| Apostles | Grace | Saint |
| Blessed Mother | Holy Spirit | Scripture |
| Communion | Mercy | Sin |
| Eucharist | Prayer | Trinity |
| Faith | Reconciliation | Trust |
| Forgiveness | Sacrament | Virtue |

Lord,
hear my prayer!

_____

_____

_____

## Go Forth!

☐ Received Communion devoutly

☐ Genuflected when I left the pew

☐ Blessed myself with Holy Water when I left

☐ Showed mercy to someone today

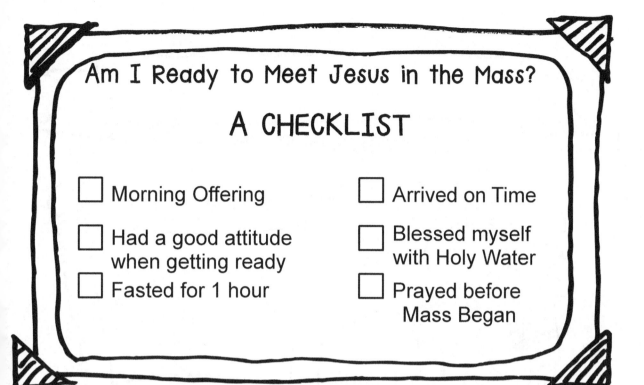

# Am I Ready to Meet Jesus in the Mass?

## A CHECKLIST

- ☐ Morning Offering
- ☐ Had a good attitude when getting ready
- ☐ Fasted for 1 hour

- ☐ Arrived on Time
- ☐ Blessed myself with Holy Water
- ☐ Prayed before Mass Began

Liturgical Color

Make a tally mark each time you hear the words:
"Jesus Christ"

Responsorial Psalm

Gospel Story

Draw the Gospel Story

# Words to Listen For During Mass
## Circle each word you hear.

| | | |
|---|---|---|
| Apostles | Grace | Saint |
| Blessed Mother | Holy Spirit | Scripture |
| Communion | Mercy | Sin |
| Eucharist | Prayer | Trinity |
| Faith | Reconciliation | Trust |
| Forgiveness | Sacrament | Virtue |

Lord,
hear my prayer!

_____

_____

_____

## Go Forth!

- ☐ Received Communion devoutly
- ☐ Genuflected when I left the pew
- ☐ Blessed myself with Holy Water when I left
- ☐ Showed mercy to someone today

# Am I Ready to Meet Jesus in the Mass?

## A CHECKLIST

☐ Morning Offering

☐ Had a good attitude when getting ready

☐ Fasted for 1 hour

☐ Arrived on Time

☐ Blessed myself with Holy Water

☐ Prayed before Mass Began

Liturgical Color

Make a tally mark each time you hear the words:
## "Jesus Christ"

Responsorial Psalm

Gospel Story

Draw the Gospel Story

# Words to Listen For During Mass
## Circle each word you hear.

| | | |
|---|---|---|
| Apostles | Grace | Saint |
| Blessed Mother | Holy Spirit | Scripture |
| Communion | Mercy | Sin |
| Eucharist | Prayer | Trinity |
| Faith | Reconciliation | Trust |
| Forgiveness | Sacrament | Virtue |

Lord,
hear my prayer!

_____

_____

_____

## Go Forth!

☐ Received Communion devoutly

☐ Genuflected when I left the pew

☐ Blessed myself with Holy Water when I left

☐ Showed mercy to someone today

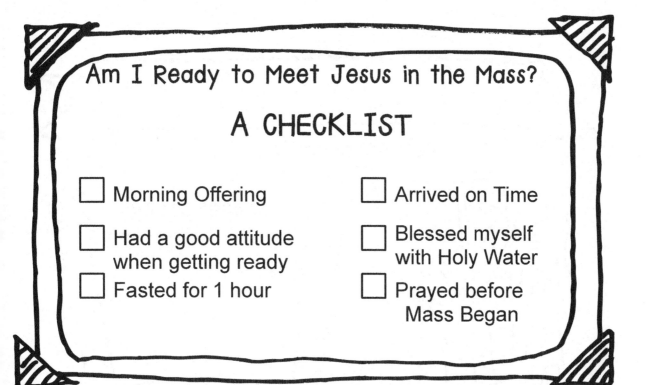

# Am I Ready to Meet Jesus in the Mass?

## A CHECKLIST

☐ Morning Offering

☐ Had a good attitude when getting ready

☐ Fasted for 1 hour

☐ Arrived on Time

☐ Blessed myself with Holy Water

☐ Prayed before Mass Began

Liturgical Color

Make a tally mark each time you hear the words:
**"Jesus Christ"**

Responsorial Psalm

Gospel Story

Draw the Gospel Story

# Words to Listen For During Mass
## Circle each word you hear.

| | | |
|---|---|---|
| Apostles | Grace | Saint |
| Blessed Mother | Holy Spirit | Scripture |
| Communion | Mercy | Sin |
| Eucharist | Prayer | Trinity |
| Faith | Reconciliation | Trust |
| Forgiveness | Sacrament | Virtue |

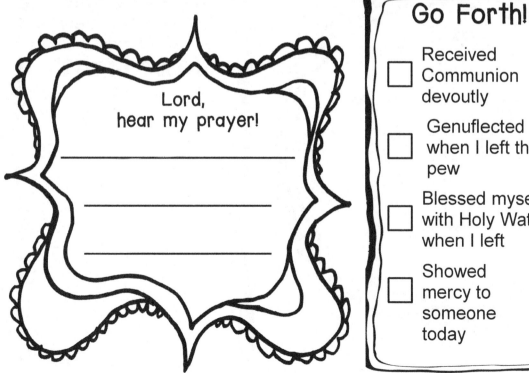

Lord,
hear my prayer!

_____

_____

_____

## Go Forth!

☐ Received Communion devoutly

☐ Genuflected when I left the pew

☐ Blessed myself with Holy Water when I left

☐ Showed mercy to someone today

# Am I Ready to Meet Jesus in the Mass?

## A CHECKLIST

☐ Morning Offering

☐ Had a good attitude when getting ready

☐ Fasted for 1 hour

☐ Arrived on Time

☐ Blessed myself with Holy Water

☐ Prayed before Mass Began

Liturgical Color

Make a tally mark each time you hear the words: "Jesus Christ"

Responsorial Psalm

Gospel Story

Draw the Gospel Story

# Words to Listen For During Mass
## Circle each word you hear.

| | | |
|---|---|---|
| Apostles | Grace | Saint |
| Blessed Mother | Holy Spirit | Scripture |
| Communion | Mercy | Sin |
| Eucharist | Prayer | Trinity |
| Faith | Reconciliation | Trust |
| Forgiveness | Sacrament | Virtue |

Lord,
hear my prayer!

_____

_____

_____

## Go Forth!

☐ Received Communion devoutly

☐ Genuflected when I left the pew

☐ Blessed myself with Holy Water when I left

☐ Showed mercy to someone today

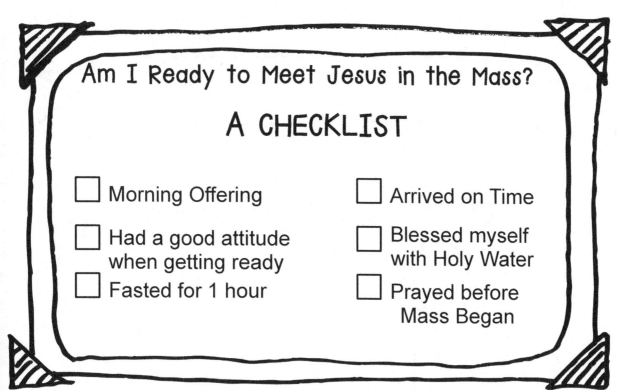

# Am I Ready to Meet Jesus in the Mass?

## A CHECKLIST

- ☐ Morning Offering
- ☐ Had a good attitude when getting ready
- ☐ Fasted for 1 hour

- ☐ Arrived on Time
- ☐ Blessed myself with Holy Water
- ☐ Prayed before Mass Began

Liturgical Color

Make a tally mark each time you hear the words:
"Jesus Christ"

Responsorial Psalm

Gospel Story

Draw the Gospel Story

# Words to Listen For During Mass
## Circle each word you hear.

| | | |
|---|---|---|
| Apostles | Grace | Saint |
| Blessed Mother | Holy Spirit | Scripture |
| Communion | Mercy | Sin |
| Eucharist | Prayer | Trinity |
| Faith | Reconciliation | Trust |
| Forgiveness | Sacrament | Virtue |

Lord,
hear my prayer!

_____

_____

_____

## Go Forth!

☐ Received Communion devoutly

☐ Genuflected when I left the pew

☐ Blessed myself with Holy Water when I left

☐ Showed mercy to someone today

# Am I Ready to Meet Jesus in the Mass?

## A CHECKLIST

☐ Morning Offering

☐ Had a good attitude when getting ready

☐ Fasted for 1 hour

☐ Arrived on Time

☐ Blessed myself with Holy Water

☐ Prayed before Mass Began

Liturgical Color

Make a tally mark each time you hear the words:
**"Jesus Christ"**

Responsorial Psalm

Gospel Story

Draw the Gospel Story

# Words to Listen For During Mass
## Circle each word you hear.

| | | |
|---|---|---|
| Apostles | Grace | Saint |
| Blessed Mother | Holy Spirit | Scripture |
| Communion | Mercy | Sin |
| Eucharist | Prayer | Trinity |
| Faith | Reconciliation | Trust |
| Forgiveness | Sacrament | Virtue |

Lord,
hear my prayer!

_____

_____

_____

## Go Forth!

☐ Received Communion devoutly

☐ Genuflected when I left the pew

☐ Blessed myself with Holy Water when I left

☐ Showed mercy to someone today

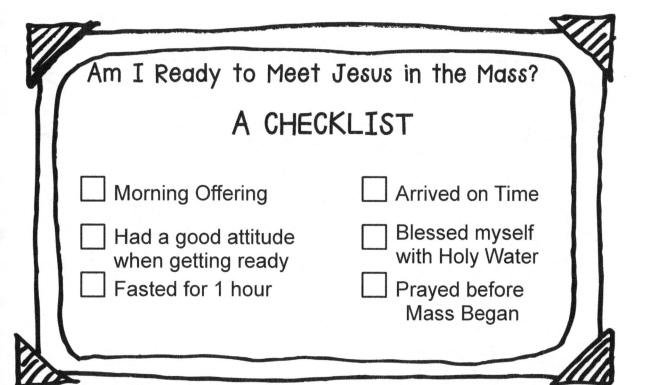

# Am I Ready to Meet Jesus in the Mass?

## A CHECKLIST

☐ Morning Offering

☐ Had a good attitude when getting ready

☐ Fasted for 1 hour

☐ Arrived on Time

☐ Blessed myself with Holy Water

☐ Prayed before Mass Began

Liturgical Color

Make a tally mark each time you hear the words:
**"Jesus Christ"**

Responsorial Psalm

Gospel Story

Draw the Gospel Story

# Words to Listen For During Mass
## Circle each word you hear.

| | | |
|---|---|---|
| Apostles | Grace | Saint |
| Blessed Mother | Holy Spirit | Scripture |
| Communion | Mercy | Sin |
| Eucharist | Prayer | Trinity |
| Faith | Reconciliation | Trust |
| Forgiveness | Sacrament | Virtue |

Lord,
hear my prayer!

_____

_____

_____

## Go Forth!

- ☐ Received Communion devoutly
- ☐ Genuflected when I left the pew
- ☐ Blessed myself with Holy Water when I left
- ☐ Showed mercy to someone today

# Am I Ready to Meet Jesus in the Mass?

## A CHECKLIST

- ☐ Morning Offering
- ☐ Had a good attitude when getting ready
- ☐ Fasted for 1 hour

- ☐ Arrived on Time
- ☐ Blessed myself with Holy Water
- ☐ Prayed before Mass Began

Liturgical Color

Make a tally mark each time you hear the words:
**"Jesus Christ"**

Responsorial Psalm

Gospel Story

Draw the Gospel Story

# Words to Listen For During Mass
## Circle each word you hear.

| | | |
|---|---|---|
| Apostles | Grace | Saint |
| Blessed Mother | Holy Spirit | Scripture |
| Communion | Mercy | Sin |
| Eucharist | Prayer | Trinity |
| Faith | Reconciliation | Trust |
| Forgiveness | Sacrament | Virtue |

Lord,
hear my prayer!

_____

_____

_____

## Go Forth!

- ☐ Received Communion devoutly
- ☐ Genuflected when I left the pew
- ☐ Blessed myself with Holy Water when I left
- ☐ Showed mercy to someone today

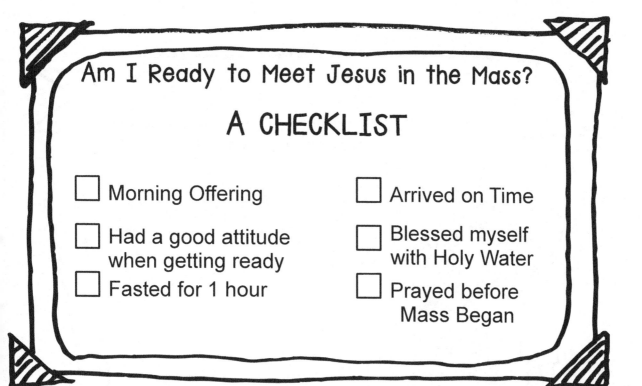

# Am I Ready to Meet Jesus in the Mass?

## A CHECKLIST

☐ Morning Offering

☐ Had a good attitude when getting ready

☐ Fasted for 1 hour

☐ Arrived on Time

☐ Blessed myself with Holy Water

☐ Prayed before Mass Began

Liturgical Color

Make a tally mark each time you hear the words:
**"Jesus Christ"**

Responsorial Psalm

Gospel Story

Draw the Gospel Story

# Words to Listen For During Mass
## Circle each word you hear.

| | | |
|---|---|---|
| Apostles | Grace | Saint |
| Blessed Mother | Holy Spirit | Scripture |
| Communion | Mercy | Sin |
| Eucharist | Prayer | Trinity |
| Faith | Reconciliation | Trust |
| Forgiveness | Sacrament | Virtue |

Lord,
hear my prayer!

_____

_____

_____

## Go Forth!

☐ Received Communion devoutly

☐ Genuflected when I left the pew

☐ Blessed myself with Holy Water when I left

☐ Showed mercy to someone today

# Am I Ready to Meet Jesus in the Mass?

## A CHECKLIST

☐ Morning Offering

☐ Had a good attitude when getting ready

☐ Fasted for 1 hour

☐ Arrived on Time

☐ Blessed myself with Holy Water

☐ Prayed before Mass Began

Liturgical Color

Make a tally mark each time you hear the words:
**"Jesus Christ"**

Responsorial Psalm

Gospel Story

Draw the Gospel Story

# Words to Listen For During Mass
## Circle each word you hear.

| | | |
|---|---|---|
| Apostles | Grace | Saint |
| Blessed Mother | Holy Spirit | Scripture |
| Communion | Mercy | Sin |
| Eucharist | Prayer | Trinity |
| Faith | Reconciliation | Trust |
| Forgiveness | Sacrament | Virtue |

Lord,
hear my prayer!

_____

_____

_____

## Go Forth!

☐ Received Communion devoutly

☐ Genuflected when I left the pew

☐ Blessed myself with Holy Water when I left

☐ Showed mercy to someone today

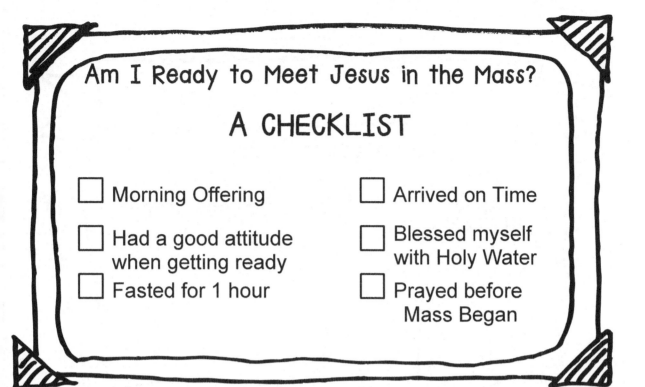

# Am I Ready to Meet Jesus in the Mass?

## A CHECKLIST

☐ Morning Offering

☐ Had a good attitude when getting ready

☐ Fasted for 1 hour

☐ Arrived on Time

☐ Blessed myself with Holy Water

☐ Prayed before Mass Began

Liturgical Color

Make a tally mark each time you hear the words:
**"Jesus Christ"**

Responsorial Psalm

Gospel Story

Draw the Gospel Story

# Words to Listen For During Mass
## Circle each word you hear.

| | | |
|---|---|---|
| Apostles | Grace | Saint |
| Blessed Mother | Holy Spirit | Scripture |
| Communion | Mercy | Sin |
| Eucharist | Prayer | Trinity |
| Faith | Reconciliation | Trust |
| Forgiveness | Sacrament | Virtue |

Lord,
hear my prayer!

_____

_____

_____

## Go Forth!

☐ Received Communion devoutly

☐ Genuflected when I left the pew

☐ Blessed myself with Holy Water when I left

☐ Showed mercy to someone today

# Am I Ready to Meet Jesus in the Mass?

## A CHECKLIST

☐ Morning Offering

☐ Had a good attitude when getting ready

☐ Fasted for 1 hour

☐ Arrived on Time

☐ Blessed myself with Holy Water

☐ Prayed before Mass Began

Liturgical Color

Make a tally mark each time you hear the words:
**"Jesus Christ"**

Responsorial Psalm

Gospel Story

Draw the Gospel Story

# Words to Listen For During Mass
## Circle each word you hear.

| | | |
|---|---|---|
| Apostles | Grace | Saint |
| Blessed Mother | Holy Spirit | Scripture |
| Communion | Mercy | Sin |
| Eucharist | Prayer | Trinity |
| Faith | Reconciliation | Trust |
| Forgiveness | Sacrament | Virtue |

Lord,
hear my prayer!

_____

_____

_____

## Go Forth!

☐ Received Communion devoutly

☐ Genuflected when I left the pew

☐ Blessed myself with Holy Water when I left

☐ Showed mercy to someone today

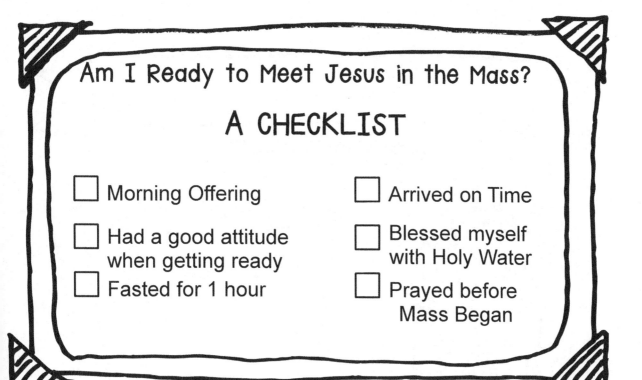

# Am I Ready to Meet Jesus in the Mass?

## A CHECKLIST

☐ Morning Offering

☐ Had a good attitude when getting ready

☐ Fasted for 1 hour

☐ Arrived on Time

☐ Blessed myself with Holy Water

☐ Prayed before Mass Began

Liturgical Color

Make a tally mark each time you hear the words:
**"Jesus Christ"**

Responsorial Psalm

Gospel Story

Draw the Gospel Story

# Words to Listen For During Mass
## Circle each word you hear.

| | | |
|---|---|---|
| Apostles | Grace | Saint |
| Blessed Mother | Holy Spirit | Scripture |
| Communion | Mercy | Sin |
| Eucharist | Prayer | Trinity |
| Faith | Reconciliation | Trust |
| Forgiveness | Sacrament | Virtue |

Lord,
hear my prayer!

_____

_____

_____

## Go Forth!

☐ Received Communion devoutly

☐ Genuflected when I left the pew

☐ Blessed myself with Holy Water when I left

☐ Showed mercy to someone today

# Am I Ready to Meet Jesus in the Mass?

## A CHECKLIST

☐ Morning Offering

☐ Had a good attitude when getting ready

☐ Fasted for 1 hour

☐ Arrived on Time

☐ Blessed myself with Holy Water

☐ Prayed before Mass Began

Liturgical Color

Make a tally mark each time you hear the words:
**"Jesus Christ"**

Responsorial Psalm

Gospel Story

Draw the Gospel Story

# Words to Listen For During Mass
## Circle each word you hear.

| | | |
|---|---|---|
| Apostles | Grace | Saint |
| Blessed Mother | Holy Spirit | Scripture |
| Communion | Mercy | Sin |
| Eucharist | Prayer | Trinity |
| Faith | Reconciliation | Trust |
| Forgiveness | Sacrament | Virtue |

Lord,
hear my prayer!

_____

_____

_____

## Go Forth!

- ☐ Received Communion devoutly
- ☐ Genuflected when I left the pew
- ☐ Blessed myself with Holy Water when I left
- ☐ Showed mercy to someone today

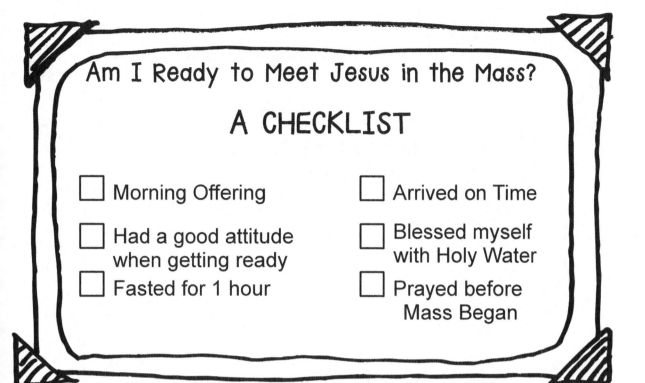

# Am I Ready to Meet Jesus in the Mass?

## A CHECKLIST

☐ Morning Offering

☐ Had a good attitude when getting ready

☐ Fasted for 1 hour

☐ Arrived on Time

☐ Blessed myself with Holy Water

☐ Prayed before Mass Began

Liturgical Color

Make a tally mark each time you hear the words:
**"Jesus Christ"**

Responsorial Psalm

Gospel Story

Draw the Gospel Story

# Words to Listen For During Mass
## Circle each word you hear.

| | | |
|---|---|---|
| Apostles | Grace | Saint |
| Blessed Mother | Holy Spirit | Scripture |
| Communion | Mercy | Sin |
| Eucharist | Prayer | Trinity |
| Faith | Reconciliation | Trust |
| Forgiveness | Sacrament | Virtue |

Lord,
hear my prayer!

_____

_____

_____

## Go Forth!

☐ Received Communion devoutly

☐ Genuflected when I left the pew

☐ Blessed myself with Holy Water when I left

☐ Showed mercy to someone today

# Am I Ready to Meet Jesus in the Mass?

## A CHECKLIST

- [ ] Morning Offering
- [ ] Had a good attitude when getting ready
- [ ] Fasted for 1 hour

- [ ] Arrived on Time
- [ ] Blessed myself with Holy Water
- [ ] Prayed before Mass Began

Liturgical Color

Make a tally mark each time you hear the words:
**"Jesus Christ"**

Responsorial Psalm

Gospel Story

Draw the Gospel Story

# Words to Listen For During Mass
## Circle each word you hear.

| | | |
|---|---|---|
| Apostles | Grace | Saint |
| Blessed Mother | Holy Spirit | Scripture |
| Communion | Mercy | Sin |
| Eucharist | Prayer | Trinity |
| Faith | Reconciliation | Trust |
| Forgiveness | Sacrament | Virtue |

Lord,
hear my prayer!

_____

_____

_____

## Go Forth!

☐ Received Communion devoutly

☐ Genuflected when I left the pew

☐ Blessed myself with Holy Water when I left

☐ Showed mercy to someone today

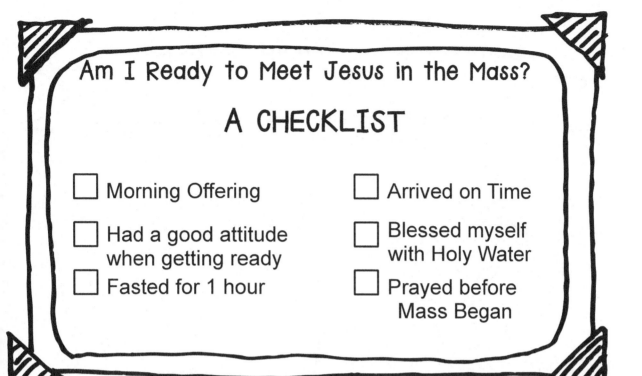

# Am I Ready to Meet Jesus in the Mass?

## A CHECKLIST

☐ Morning Offering

☐ Had a good attitude when getting ready

☐ Fasted for 1 hour

☐ Arrived on Time

☐ Blessed myself with Holy Water

☐ Prayed before Mass Began

Liturgical Color

Make a tally mark each time you hear the words:
**"Jesus Christ"**

Responsorial Psalm

Gospel Story

Draw the Gospel Story

# Words to Listen For During Mass
## Circle each word you hear.

| | | |
|---|---|---|
| Apostles | Grace | Saint |
| Blessed Mother | Holy Spirit | Scripture |
| Communion | Mercy | Sin |
| Eucharist | Prayer | Trinity |
| Faith | Reconciliation | Trust |
| Forgiveness | Sacrament | Virtue |

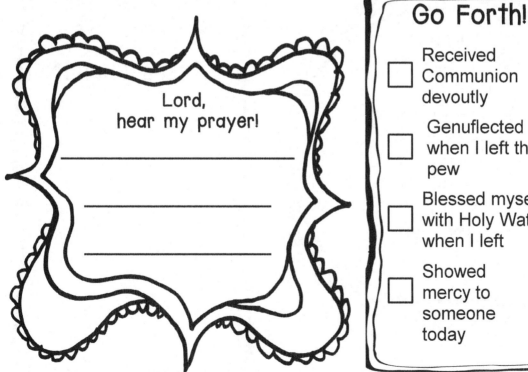

Lord,
hear my prayer!

_____

_____

_____

## Go Forth!

☐ Received Communion devoutly

☐ Genuflected when I left the pew

☐ Blessed myself with Holy Water when I left

☐ Showed mercy to someone today

# Am I Ready to Meet Jesus in the Mass?

## A CHECKLIST

☐ Morning Offering

☐ Had a good attitude when getting ready

☐ Fasted for 1 hour

☐ Arrived on Time

☐ Blessed myself with Holy Water

☐ Prayed before Mass Began

Liturgical Color

Make a tally mark each time you hear the words:
**"Jesus Christ"**

Responsorial Psalm

Gospel Story

Draw the Gospel Story

# Words to Listen For During Mass
## Circle each word you hear.

| | | |
|---|---|---|
| Apostles | Grace | Saint |
| Blessed Mother | Holy Spirit | Scripture |
| Communion | Mercy | Sin |
| Eucharist | Prayer | Trinity |
| Faith | Reconciliation | Trust |
| Forgiveness | Sacrament | Virtue |

Lord,
hear my prayer!

_____

_____

_____

## Go Forth!

- ☐ Received Communion devoutly
- ☐ Genuflected when I left the pew
- ☐ Blessed myself with Holy Water when I left
- ☐ Showed mercy to someone today

## Am I Ready to Meet Jesus in the Mass?

## A CHECKLIST

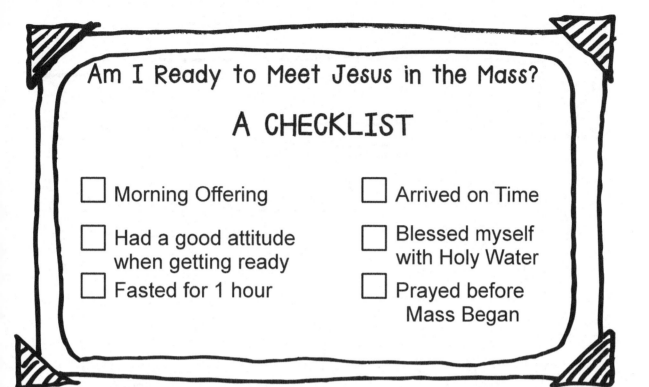

☐ Morning Offering

☐ Had a good attitude when getting ready

☐ Fasted for 1 hour

☐ Arrived on Time

☐ Blessed myself with Holy Water

☐ Prayed before Mass Began

Liturgical Color

Make a tally mark each time you hear the words:
"Jesus Christ"

Responsorial Psalm

Gospel Story

Draw the Gospel Story

# Words to Listen For During Mass
## Circle each word you hear.

| | | |
|---|---|---|
| Apostles | Grace | Saint |
| Blessed Mother | Holy Spirit | Scripture |
| Communion | Mercy | Sin |
| Eucharist | Prayer | Trinity |
| Faith | Reconciliation | Trust |
| Forgiveness | Sacrament | Virtue |

Lord,
hear my prayer!

_____

_____

_____

## Go Forth!

☐ Received Communion devoutly

☐ Genuflected when I left the pew

☐ Blessed myself with Holy Water when I left

☐ Showed mercy to someone today

# Am I Ready to Meet Jesus in the Mass?

## A CHECKLIST

☐ Morning Offering

☐ Had a good attitude when getting ready

☐ Fasted for 1 hour

☐ Arrived on Time

☐ Blessed myself with Holy Water

☐ Prayed before Mass Began

Liturgical Color

Make a tally mark each time you hear the words:
**"Jesus Christ"**

Responsorial Psalm

Gospel Story

Draw the Gospel Story

# Words to Listen For During Mass
## Circle each word you hear.

| | | |
|---|---|---|
| Apostles | Grace | Saint |
| Blessed Mother | Holy Spirit | Scripture |
| Communion | Mercy | Sin |
| Eucharist | Prayer | Trinity |
| Faith | Reconciliation | Trust |
| Forgiveness | Sacrament | Virtue |

Lord,
hear my prayer!

_____

_____

_____

## Go Forth!

- ☐ Received Communion devoutly
- ☐ Genuflected when I left the pew
- ☐ Blessed myself with Holy Water when I left
- ☐ Showed mercy to someone today

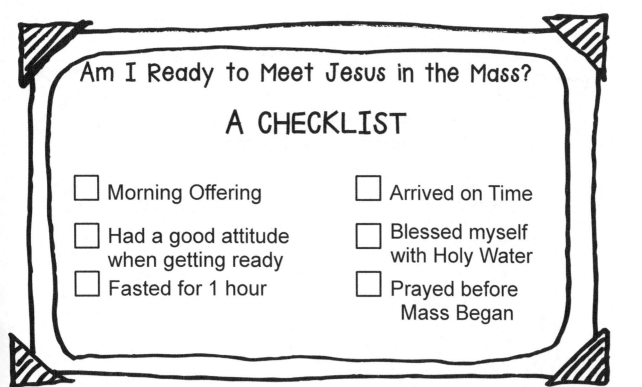

# Am I Ready to Meet Jesus in the Mass?

## A CHECKLIST

- ☐ Morning Offering
- ☐ Had a good attitude when getting ready
- ☐ Fasted for 1 hour

- ☐ Arrived on Time
- ☐ Blessed myself with Holy Water
- ☐ Prayed before Mass Began

Liturgical Color

Make a tally mark each time you hear the words:

**"Jesus Christ"**

Responsorial Psalm

Gospel Story

Draw the Gospel Story

# Words to Listen For During Mass
## Circle each word you hear.

| | | |
|---|---|---|
| Apostles | Grace | Saint |
| Blessed Mother | Holy Spirit | Scripture |
| Communion | Mercy | Sin |
| Eucharist | Prayer | Trinity |
| Faith | Reconciliation | Trust |
| Forgiveness | Sacrament | Virtue |

Lord,
hear my prayer!

_____

_____

_____

## Go Forth!

☐ Received Communion devoutly

☐ Genuflected when I left the pew

☐ Blessed myself with Holy Water when I left

☐ Showed mercy to someone today

# Am I Ready to Meet Jesus in the Mass?

## A CHECKLIST

☐ Morning Offering

☐ Had a good attitude when getting ready

☐ Fasted for 1 hour

☐ Arrived on Time

☐ Blessed myself with Holy Water

☐ Prayed before Mass Began

Liturgical Color

Make a tally mark each time you hear the words:
## "Jesus Christ"

Responsorial Psalm

Gospel Story

Draw the Gospel Story

# Words to Listen For During Mass
## Circle each word you hear.

| | | |
|---|---|---|
| Apostles | Grace | Saint |
| Blessed Mother | Holy Spirit | Scripture |
| Communion | Mercy | Sin |
| Eucharist | Prayer | Trinity |
| Faith | Reconciliation | Trust |
| Forgiveness | Sacrament | Virtue |

Lord,
hear my prayer!

_____

_____

_____

## Go Forth!

☐ Received Communion devoutly

☐ Genuflected when I left the pew

☐ Blessed myself with Holy Water when I left

☐ Showed mercy to someone today

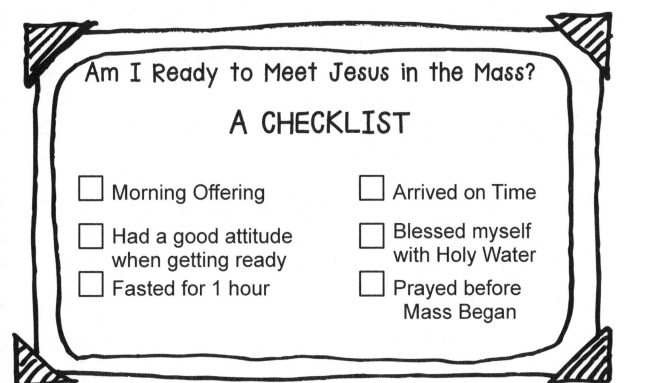

# Am I Ready to Meet Jesus in the Mass?

## A CHECKLIST

☐ Morning Offering

☐ Had a good attitude when getting ready

☐ Fasted for 1 hour

☐ Arrived on Time

☐ Blessed myself with Holy Water

☐ Prayed before Mass Began

Liturgical Color

Make a tally mark each time you hear the words:

**"Jesus Christ"**

Responsorial Psalm

Gospel Story

Draw the Gospel Story

# Words to Listen For During Mass
## Circle each word you hear.

| | | |
|---|---|---|
| Apostles | Grace | Saint |
| Blessed Mother | Holy Spirit | Scripture |
| Communion | Mercy | Sin |
| Eucharist | Prayer | Trinity |
| Faith | Reconciliation | Trust |
| Forgiveness | Sacrament | Virtue |

Lord,
hear my prayer!

_____

_____

_____

## Go Forth!

☐ Received Communion devoutly

☐ Genuflected when I left the pew

☐ Blessed myself with Holy Water when I left

☐ Showed mercy to someone today

# Am I Ready to Meet Jesus in the Mass?

## A CHECKLIST

- ☐ Morning Offering
- ☐ Had a good attitude when getting ready
- ☐ Fasted for 1 hour
- ☐ Arrived on Time
- ☐ Blessed myself with Holy Water
- ☐ Prayed before Mass Began

Liturgical Color

Make a tally mark each time you hear the words:
**"Jesus Christ"**

Responsorial Psalm

Gospel Story

Draw the Gospel Story

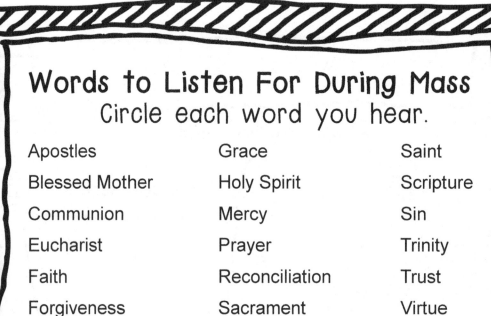

# Words to Listen For During Mass
## Circle each word you hear.

| | | |
|---|---|---|
| Apostles | Grace | Saint |
| Blessed Mother | Holy Spirit | Scripture |
| Communion | Mercy | Sin |
| Eucharist | Prayer | Trinity |
| Faith | Reconciliation | Trust |
| Forgiveness | Sacrament | Virtue |

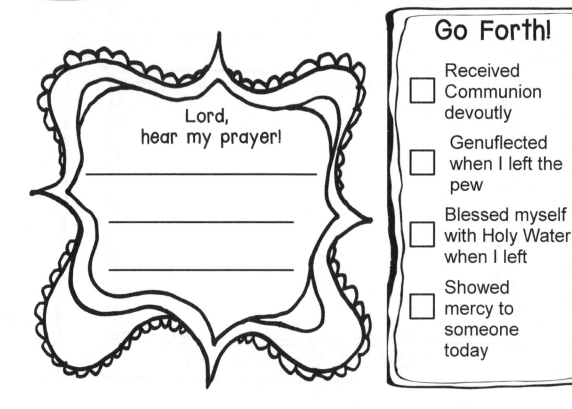

Lord,
hear my prayer!

_____

_____

_____

## Go Forth!

☐ Received Communion devoutly

☐ Genuflected when I left the pew

☐ Blessed myself with Holy Water when I left

☐ Showed mercy to someone today

# Am I Ready to Meet Jesus in the Mass?

## A CHECKLIST

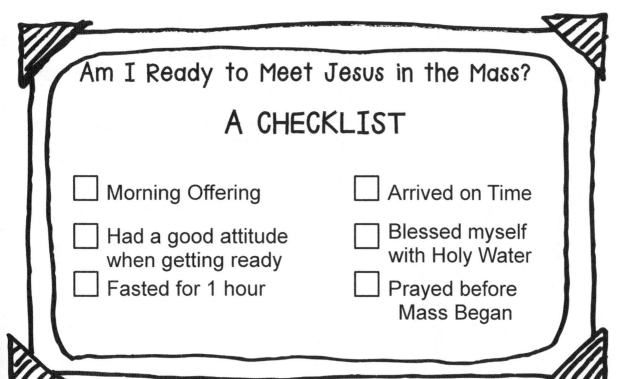

☐ Morning Offering

☐ Had a good attitude when getting ready

☐ Fasted for 1 hour

☐ Arrived on Time

☐ Blessed myself with Holy Water

☐ Prayed before Mass Began

Liturgical Color

Make a tally mark each time you hear the words:
**"Jesus Christ"**

Responsorial Psalm

Gospel Story

Draw the Gospel Story

# Words to Listen For During Mass
## Circle each word you hear.

| | | |
|---|---|---|
| Apostles | Grace | Saint |
| Blessed Mother | Holy Spirit | Scripture |
| Communion | Mercy | Sin |
| Eucharist | Prayer | Trinity |
| Faith | Reconciliation | Trust |
| Forgiveness | Sacrament | Virtue |

Lord,
hear my prayer!

_____

_____

_____

## Go Forth!

☐ Received Communion devoutly

☐ Genuflected when I left the pew

☐ Blessed myself with Holy Water when I left

☐ Showed mercy to someone today

# Am I Ready to Meet Jesus in the Mass?

## A CHECKLIST

☐ Morning Offering

☐ Had a good attitude when getting ready

☐ Fasted for 1 hour

☐ Arrived on Time

☐ Blessed myself with Holy Water

☐ Prayed before Mass Began

Liturgical Color

Make a tally mark each time you hear the words:
**"Jesus Christ"**

Responsorial Psalm

Gospel Story

Draw the Gospel Story

# Words to Listen For During Mass
## Circle each word you hear.

| | | |
|---|---|---|
| Apostles | Grace | Saint |
| Blessed Mother | Holy Spirit | Scripture |
| Communion | Mercy | Sin |
| Eucharist | Prayer | Trinity |
| Faith | Reconciliation | Trust |
| Forgiveness | Sacrament | Virtue |

Lord,
hear my prayer!

_____

_____

_____

## Go Forth!

☐ Received Communion devoutly

☐ Genuflected when I left the pew

☐ Blessed myself with Holy Water when I left

☐ Showed mercy to someone today

# Am I Ready to Meet Jesus in the Mass?

## A CHECKLIST

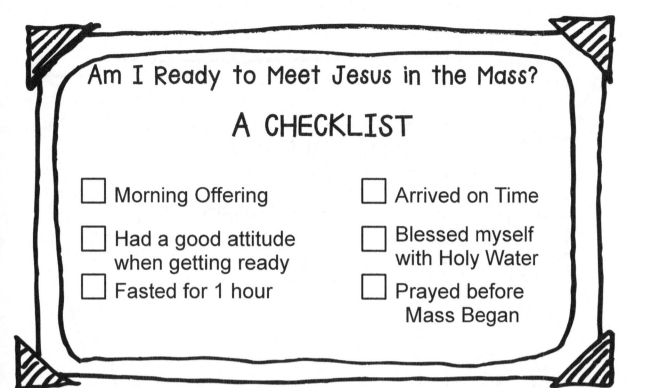

- ☐ Morning Offering
- ☐ Had a good attitude when getting ready
- ☐ Fasted for 1 hour
- ☐ Arrived on Time
- ☐ Blessed myself with Holy Water
- ☐ Prayed before Mass Began

Liturgical Color

Make a tally mark each time you hear the words:
"Jesus Christ"

Responsorial Psalm

Gospel Story

Draw the Gospel Story

# Words to Listen For During Mass
## Circle each word you hear.

| | | |
|---|---|---|
| Apostles | Grace | Saint |
| Blessed Mother | Holy Spirit | Scripture |
| Communion | Mercy | Sin |
| Eucharist | Prayer | Trinity |
| Faith | Reconciliation | Trust |
| Forgiveness | Sacrament | Virtue |

Lord,
hear my prayer!

_____

_____

_____

## Go Forth!

☐ Received Communion devoutly

☐ Genuflected when I left the pew

☐ Blessed myself with Holy Water when I left

☐ Showed mercy to someone today

# Am I Ready to Meet Jesus in the Mass?

## A CHECKLIST

☐ Morning Offering

☐ Had a good attitude when getting ready

☐ Fasted for 1 hour

☐ Arrived on Time

☐ Blessed myself with Holy Water

☐ Prayed before Mass Began

Liturgical Color

Make a tally mark each time you hear the words:
**"Jesus Christ"**

Responsorial Psalm

Gospel Story

Draw the Gospel Story

# Words to Listen For During Mass
## Circle each word you hear.

| | | |
|---|---|---|
| Apostles | Grace | Saint |
| Blessed Mother | Holy Spirit | Scripture |
| Communion | Mercy | Sin |
| Eucharist | Prayer | Trinity |
| Faith | Reconciliation | Trust |
| Forgiveness | Sacrament | Virtue |

Lord,
hear my prayer!

_____

_____

_____

## Go Forth!

☐ Received Communion devoutly

☐ Genuflected when I left the pew

☐ Blessed myself with Holy Water when I left

☐ Showed mercy to someone today

# Am I Ready to Meet Jesus in the Mass?

## A CHECKLIST

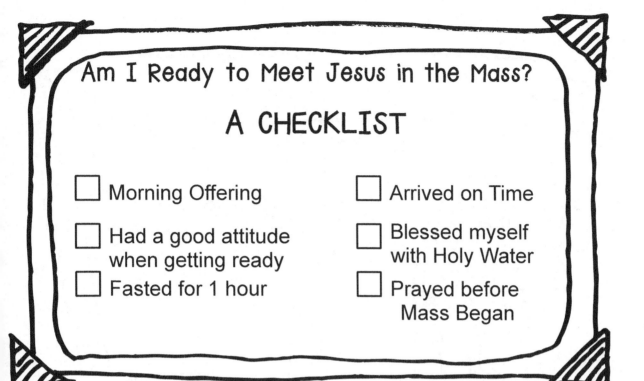

☐ Morning Offering

☐ Had a good attitude when getting ready

☐ Fasted for 1 hour

☐ Arrived on Time

☐ Blessed myself with Holy Water

☐ Prayed before Mass Began

Liturgical Color

Make a tally mark each time you hear the words: "Jesus Christ"

Responsorial Psalm

Gospel Story

Draw the Gospel Story

# Words to Listen For During Mass
## Circle each word you hear.

| | | |
|---|---|---|
| Apostles | Grace | Saint |
| Blessed Mother | Holy Spirit | Scripture |
| Communion | Mercy | Sin |
| Eucharist | Prayer | Trinity |
| Faith | Reconciliation | Trust |
| Forgiveness | Sacrament | Virtue |

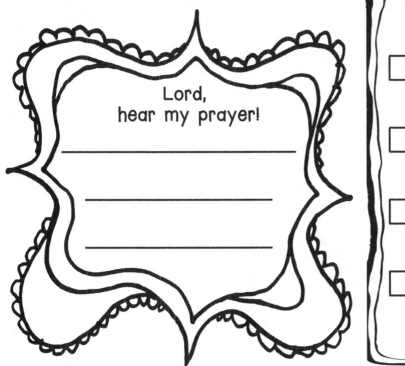

Lord,
hear my prayer!

_____

_____

_____

# Go Forth!

☐ Received Communion devoutly

☐ Genuflected when I left the pew

☐ Blessed myself with Holy Water when I left

☐ Showed mercy to someone today

## Am I Ready to Meet Jesus in the Mass?

## A CHECKLIST

- ☐ Morning Offering
- ☐ Had a good attitude when getting ready
- ☐ Fasted for 1 hour

- ☐ Arrived on Time
- ☐ Blessed myself with Holy Water
- ☐ Prayed before Mass Began

Liturgical Color

Make a tally mark each time you hear the words:
**"Jesus Christ"**

Responsorial Psalm

Gospel Story

Draw the Gospel Story

# Words to Listen For During Mass
## Circle each word you hear.

| | | |
|---|---|---|
| Apostles | Grace | Saint |
| Blessed Mother | Holy Spirit | Scripture |
| Communion | Mercy | Sin |
| Eucharist | Prayer | Trinity |
| Faith | Reconciliation | Trust |
| Forgiveness | Sacrament | Virtue |

Lord,
hear my prayer!

_____

_____

_____

## Go Forth!

☐ Received Communion devoutly

☐ Genuflected when I left the pew

☐ Blessed myself with Holy Water when I left

☐ Showed mercy to someone today

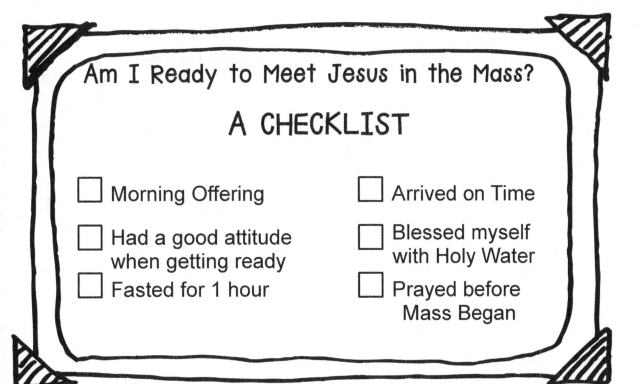

# Am I Ready to Meet Jesus in the Mass?

## A CHECKLIST

- ☐ Morning Offering
- ☐ Had a good attitude when getting ready
- ☐ Fasted for 1 hour

- ☐ Arrived on Time
- ☐ Blessed myself with Holy Water
- ☐ Prayed before Mass Began

Liturgical Color

Make a tally mark each time you hear the words:
**"Jesus Christ"**

Responsorial Psalm

Gospel Story

Draw the Gospel Story

# Words to Listen For During Mass
## Circle each word you hear.

| | | |
|---|---|---|
| Apostles | Grace | Saint |
| Blessed Mother | Holy Spirit | Scripture |
| Communion | Mercy | Sin |
| Eucharist | Prayer | Trinity |
| Faith | Reconciliation | Trust |
| Forgiveness | Sacrament | Virtue |

Lord,
hear my prayer!

_____

_____

_____

## Go Forth!

☐ Received Communion devoutly

☐ Genuflected when I left the pew

☐ Blessed myself with Holy Water when I left

☐ Showed mercy to someone today

# Am I Ready to Meet Jesus in the Mass?

## A CHECKLIST

☐ Morning Offering

☐ Had a good attitude when getting ready

☐ Fasted for 1 hour

☐ Arrived on Time

☐ Blessed myself with Holy Water

☐ Prayed before Mass Began

Liturgical Color

Make a tally mark each time you hear the words:
**"Jesus Christ"**

Responsorial Psalm

Gospel Story

Draw the Gospel Story

# Words to Listen For During Mass
## Circle each word you hear.

| | | |
|---|---|---|
| Apostles | Grace | Saint |
| Blessed Mother | Holy Spirit | Scripture |
| Communion | Mercy | Sin |
| Eucharist | Prayer | Trinity |
| Faith | Reconciliation | Trust |
| Forgiveness | Sacrament | Virtue |

Lord,
hear my prayer!

_____

_____

_____

## Go Forth!

☐ Received Communion devoutly

☐ Genuflected when I left the pew

☐ Blessed myself with Holy Water when I left

☐ Showed mercy to someone today

## Am I Ready to Meet Jesus in the Mass?

# A CHECKLIST

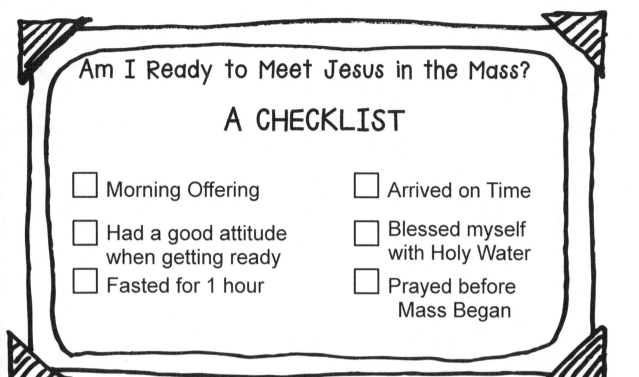

☐ Morning Offering

☐ Had a good attitude when getting ready

☐ Fasted for 1 hour

☐ Arrived on Time

☐ Blessed myself with Holy Water

☐ Prayed before Mass Began

Liturgical Color

Make a tally mark each time you hear the words:
**"Jesus Christ"**

Responsorial Psalm

Gospel Story

Draw the Gospel Story

# Words to Listen For During Mass
## Circle each word you hear.

| | | |
|---|---|---|
| Apostles | Grace | Saint |
| Blessed Mother | Holy Spirit | Scripture |
| Communion | Mercy | Sin |
| Eucharist | Prayer | Trinity |
| Faith | Reconciliation | Trust |
| Forgiveness | Sacrament | Virtue |

Lord,
hear my prayer!

_____

_____

_____

## Go Forth!

☐ Received Communion devoutly

☐ Genuflected when I left the pew

☐ Blessed myself with Holy Water when I left

☐ Showed mercy to someone today

# Am I Ready to Meet Jesus in the Mass?

## A CHECKLIST

☐ Morning Offering

☐ Had a good attitude when getting ready

☐ Fasted for 1 hour

☐ Arrived on Time

☐ Blessed myself with Holy Water

☐ Prayed before Mass Began

Liturgical Color

Make a tally mark each time you hear the words:
## "Jesus Christ"

Responsorial Psalm

Gospel Story

Draw the Gospel Story

# Words to Listen For During Mass
## Circle each word you hear.

| | | |
|---|---|---|
| Apostles | Grace | Saint |
| Blessed Mother | Holy Spirit | Scripture |
| Communion | Mercy | Sin |
| Eucharist | Prayer | Trinity |
| Faith | Reconciliation | Trust |
| Forgiveness | Sacrament | Virtue |

Lord,
hear my prayer!

_____

_____

_____

## Go Forth!

☐ Received Communion devoutly

☐ Genuflected when I left the pew

☐ Blessed myself with Holy Water when I left

☐ Showed mercy to someone today

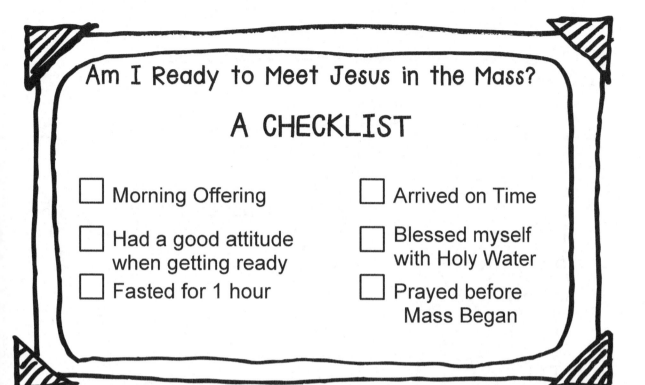

## Am I Ready to Meet Jesus in the Mass?

# A CHECKLIST

☐ Morning Offering

☐ Had a good attitude when getting ready

☐ Fasted for 1 hour

☐ Arrived on Time

☐ Blessed myself with Holy Water

☐ Prayed before Mass Began

Liturgical Color

Make a tally mark each time you hear the words:
"Jesus Christ"

Responsorial Psalm

Gospel Story

Draw the Gospel Story

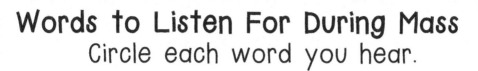

# Words to Listen For During Mass
## Circle each word you hear.

| | | |
|---|---|---|
| Apostles | Grace | Saint |
| Blessed Mother | Holy Spirit | Scripture |
| Communion | Mercy | Sin |
| Eucharist | Prayer | Trinity |
| Faith | Reconciliation | Trust |
| Forgiveness | Sacrament | Virtue |

Lord,
hear my prayer!

_____

_____

_____

## Go Forth!

☐ Received Communion devoutly

☐ Genuflected when I left the pew

☐ Blessed myself with Holy Water when I left

☐ Showed mercy to someone today

# Am I Ready to Meet Jesus in the Mass?

## A CHECKLIST

☐ Morning Offering

☐ Had a good attitude when getting ready

☐ Fasted for 1 hour

☐ Arrived on Time

☐ Blessed myself with Holy Water

☐ Prayed before Mass Began

Liturgical Color

Make a tally mark each time you hear the words:
**"Jesus Christ"**

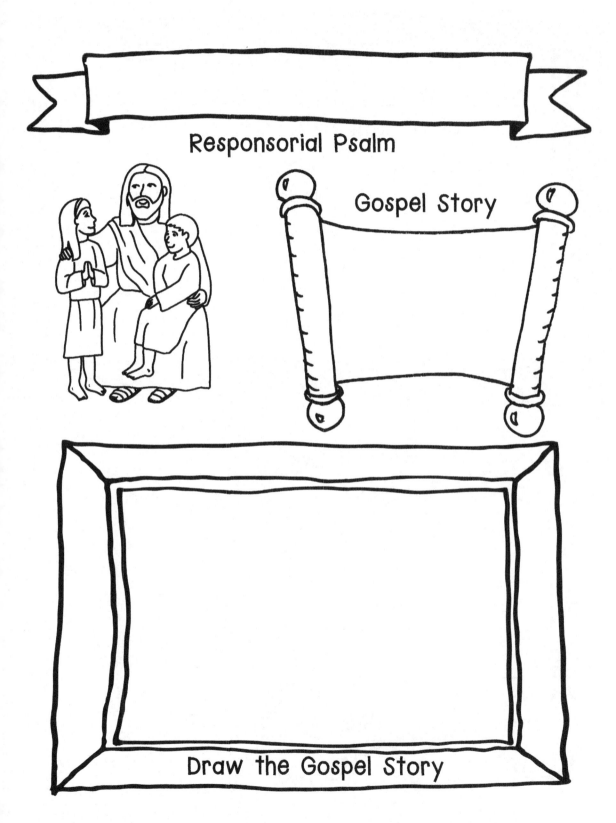

Responsorial Psalm

Gospel Story

Draw the Gospel Story

# Words to Listen For During Mass
## Circle each word you hear.

| | | |
|---|---|---|
| Apostles | Grace | Saint |
| Blessed Mother | Holy Spirit | Scripture |
| Communion | Mercy | Sin |
| Eucharist | Prayer | Trinity |
| Faith | Reconciliation | Trust |
| Forgiveness | Sacrament | Virtue |

Lord,
hear my prayer!

_____

_____

_____

## Go Forth!

☐ Received Communion devoutly

☐ Genuflected when I left the pew

☐ Blessed myself with Holy Water when I left

☐ Showed mercy to someone today

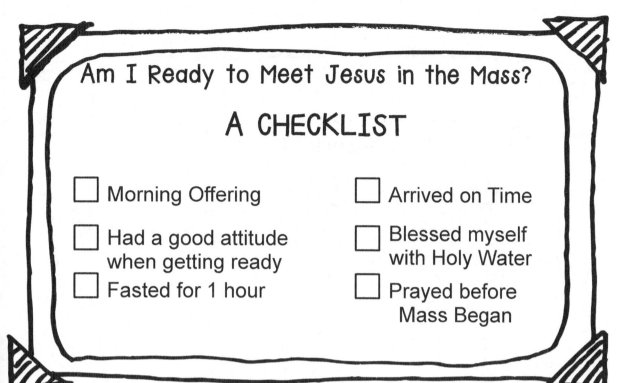

## Am I Ready to Meet Jesus in the Mass?

### A CHECKLIST

☐ Morning Offering

☐ Had a good attitude when getting ready

☐ Fasted for 1 hour

☐ Arrived on Time

☐ Blessed myself with Holy Water

☐ Prayed before Mass Began

Liturgical Color

Make a tally mark each time you hear the words:
**"Jesus Christ"**

Responsorial Psalm

Gospel Story

Draw the Gospel Story

# Words to Listen For During Mass
## Circle each word you hear.

| | | |
|---|---|---|
| Apostles | Grace | Saint |
| Blessed Mother | Holy Spirit | Scripture |
| Communion | Mercy | Sin |
| Eucharist | Prayer | Trinity |
| Faith | Reconciliation | Trust |
| Forgiveness | Sacrament | Virtue |

Lord,
hear my prayer!

_____

_____

## Go Forth!

☐ Received Communion devoutly

☐ Genuflected when I left the pew

☐ Blessed myself with Holy Water when I left

☐ Showed mercy to someone today

## Am I Ready to Meet Jesus in the Mass?

## A CHECKLIST

☐ Morning Offering

☐ Had a good attitude when getting ready

☐ Fasted for 1 hour

☐ Arrived on Time

☐ Blessed myself with Holy Water

☐ Prayed before Mass Began

Liturgical Color

Make a tally mark each time you hear the words:
**"Jesus Christ"**

Responsorial Psalm

Gospel Story

Draw the Gospel Story

# Words to Listen For During Mass
## Circle each word you hear.

| | | |
|---|---|---|
| Apostles | Grace | Saint |
| Blessed Mother | Holy Spirit | Scripture |
| Communion | Mercy | Sin |
| Eucharist | Prayer | Trinity |
| Faith | Reconciliation | Trust |
| Forgiveness | Sacrament | Virtue |

Lord,
hear my prayer!

_____

_____

_____

## Go Forth!

☐ Received Communion devoutly

☐ Genuflected when I left the pew

☐ Blessed myself with Holy Water when I left

☐ Showed mercy to someone today

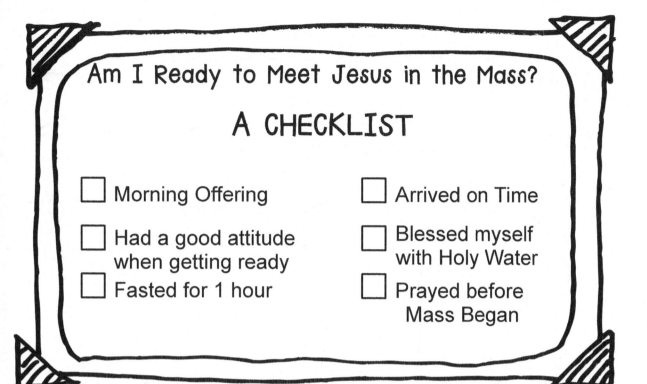

# Am I Ready to Meet Jesus in the Mass?

## A CHECKLIST

- ☐ Morning Offering
- ☐ Had a good attitude when getting ready
- ☐ Fasted for 1 hour

- ☐ Arrived on Time
- ☐ Blessed myself with Holy Water
- ☐ Prayed before Mass Began

Liturgical Color

Make a tally mark each time you hear the words:
**"Jesus Christ"**

Responsorial Psalm

Gospel Story

Draw the Gospel Story

# Words to Listen For During Mass
## Circle each word you hear.

| | | |
|---|---|---|
| Apostles | Grace | Saint |
| Blessed Mother | Holy Spirit | Scripture |
| Communion | Mercy | Sin |
| Eucharist | Prayer | Trinity |
| Faith | Reconciliation | Trust |
| Forgiveness | Sacrament | Virtue |

Lord,
hear my prayer!

_____

_____

_____

## Go Forth!

☐ Received Communion devoutly

☐ Genuflected when I left the pew

☐ Blessed myself with Holy Water when I left

☐ Showed mercy to someone today

# Am I Ready to Meet Jesus in the Mass?

## A CHECKLIST

☐ Morning Offering

☐ Had a good attitude when getting ready

☐ Fasted for 1 hour

☐ Arrived on Time

☐ Blessed myself with Holy Water

☐ Prayed before Mass Began

Liturgical Color

Make a tally mark each time you hear the words:
**"Jesus Christ"**

Responsorial Psalm

Gospel Story

Draw the Gospel Story

# Words to Listen For During Mass
## Circle each word you hear.

| | | |
|---|---|---|
| Apostles | Grace | Saint |
| Blessed Mother | Holy Spirit | Scripture |
| Communion | Mercy | Sin |
| Eucharist | Prayer | Trinity |
| Faith | Reconciliation | Trust |
| Forgiveness | Sacrament | Virtue |

Lord,
hear my prayer!

_____

_____

_____

## Go Forth!

☐ Received Communion devoutly

☐ Genuflected when I left the pew

☐ Blessed myself with Holy Water when I left

☐ Showed mercy to someone today

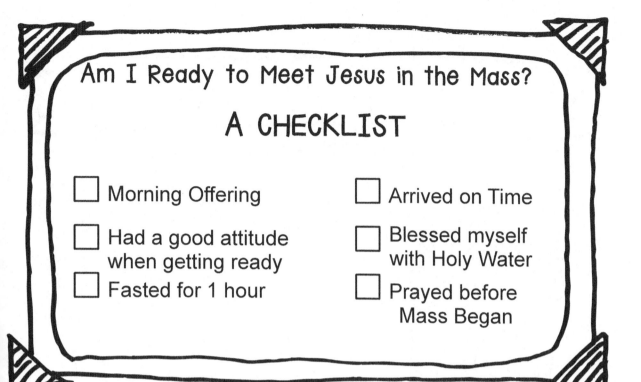

## Am I Ready to Meet Jesus in the Mass?

## A CHECKLIST

☐ Morning Offering

☐ Had a good attitude when getting ready

☐ Fasted for 1 hour

☐ Arrived on Time

☐ Blessed myself with Holy Water

☐ Prayed before Mass Began

Liturgical Color

Make a tally mark each time you hear the words:
"Jesus Christ"

Responsorial Psalm

Gospel Story

Draw the Gospel Story

# Words to Listen For During Mass
## Circle each word you hear.

| | | |
|---|---|---|
| Apostles | Grace | Saint |
| Blessed Mother | Holy Spirit | Scripture |
| Communion | Mercy | Sin |
| Eucharist | Prayer | Trinity |
| Faith | Reconciliation | Trust |
| Forgiveness | Sacrament | Virtue |

Lord,
hear my prayer!

_____

_____

_____

## Go Forth!

☐ Received Communion devoutly

☐ Genuflected when I left the pew

☐ Blessed myself with Holy Water when I left

☐ Showed mercy to someone today

# Am I Ready to Meet Jesus in the Mass?

## A CHECKLIST

☐ Morning Offering

☐ Had a good attitude when getting ready

☐ Fasted for 1 hour

☐ Arrived on Time

☐ Blessed myself with Holy Water

☐ Prayed before Mass Began

Liturgical Color

Make a tally mark each time you hear the words:
**"Jesus Christ"**

Responsorial Psalm

Gospel Story

Draw the Gospel Story

# Words to Listen For During Mass
## Circle each word you hear.

| | | |
|---|---|---|
| Apostles | Grace | Saint |
| Blessed Mother | Holy Spirit | Scripture |
| Communion | Mercy | Sin |
| Eucharist | Prayer | Trinity |
| Faith | Reconciliation | Trust |
| Forgiveness | Sacrament | Virtue |

Lord,
hear my prayer!

_____

_____

_____

## Go Forth!

☐ Received Communion devoutly

☐ Genuflected when I left the pew

☐ Blessed myself with Holy Water when I left

☐ Showed mercy to someone today

## Am I Ready to Meet Jesus in the Mass?

## A CHECKLIST

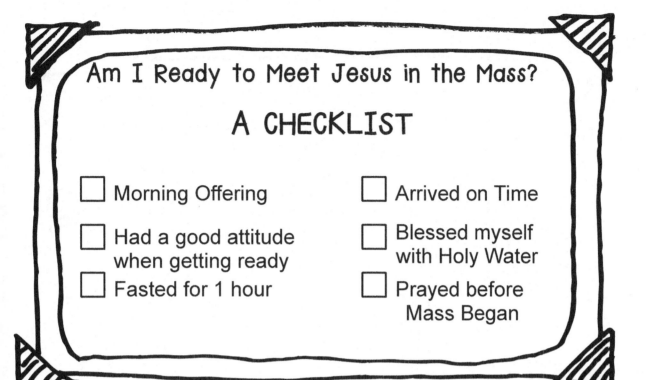

- ☐ Morning Offering
- ☐ Had a good attitude when getting ready
- ☐ Fasted for 1 hour

- ☐ Arrived on Time
- ☐ Blessed myself with Holy Water
- ☐ Prayed before Mass Began

Liturgical Color

Make a tally mark each time you hear the words:
**"Jesus Christ"**

Responsorial Psalm

Gospel Story

Draw the Gospel Story

# Words to Listen For During Mass
## Circle each word you hear.

| | | |
|---|---|---|
| Apostles | Grace | Saint |
| Blessed Mother | Holy Spirit | Scripture |
| Communion | Mercy | Sin |
| Eucharist | Prayer | Trinity |
| Faith | Reconciliation | Trust |
| Forgiveness | Sacrament | Virtue |

Lord,
hear my prayer!

_____

_____

_____

## Go Forth!

- ☐ Received Communion devoutly
- ☐ Genuflected when I left the pew
- ☐ Blessed myself with Holy Water when I left
- ☐ Showed mercy to someone today

# Am I Ready to Meet Jesus in the Mass?

## A CHECKLIST

☐ Morning Offering

☐ Had a good attitude when getting ready

☐ Fasted for 1 hour

☐ Arrived on Time

☐ Blessed myself with Holy Water

☐ Prayed before Mass Began

Liturgical Color

Make a tally mark each time you hear the words:
**"Jesus Christ"**

Responsorial Psalm

Gospel Story

Draw the Gospel Story

# Words to Listen For During Mass
## Circle each word you hear.

| | | |
|---|---|---|
| Apostles | Grace | Saint |
| Blessed Mother | Holy Spirit | Scripture |
| Communion | Mercy | Sin |
| Eucharist | Prayer | Trinity |
| Faith | Reconciliation | Trust |
| Forgiveness | Sacrament | Virtue |

Lord,
hear my prayer!

_____

_____

_____

## Go Forth!

- ☐ Received Communion devoutly
- ☐ Genuflected when I left the pew
- ☐ Blessed myself with Holy Water when I left
- ☐ Showed mercy to someone today

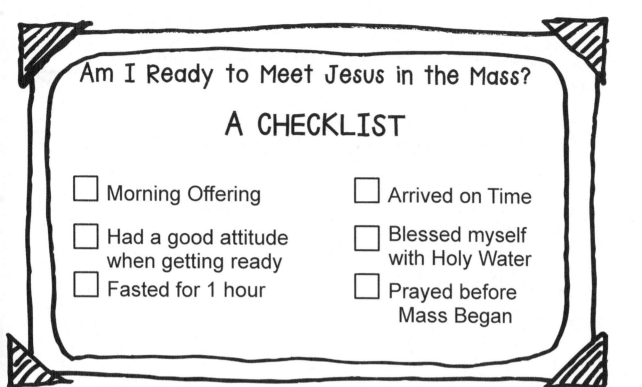

# Am I Ready to Meet Jesus in the Mass?

## A CHECKLIST

- ☐ Morning Offering
- ☐ Had a good attitude when getting ready
- ☐ Fasted for 1 hour

- ☐ Arrived on Time
- ☐ Blessed myself with Holy Water
- ☐ Prayed before Mass Began

Liturgical Color

Make a tally mark each time you hear the words:
**"Jesus Christ"**

Responsorial Psalm

Gospel Story

Draw the Gospel Story

# Words to Listen For During Mass
## Circle each word you hear.

| | | |
|---|---|---|
| Apostles | Grace | Saint |
| Blessed Mother | Holy Spirit | Scripture |
| Communion | Mercy | Sin |
| Eucharist | Prayer | Trinity |
| Faith | Reconciliation | Trust |
| Forgiveness | Sacrament | Virtue |

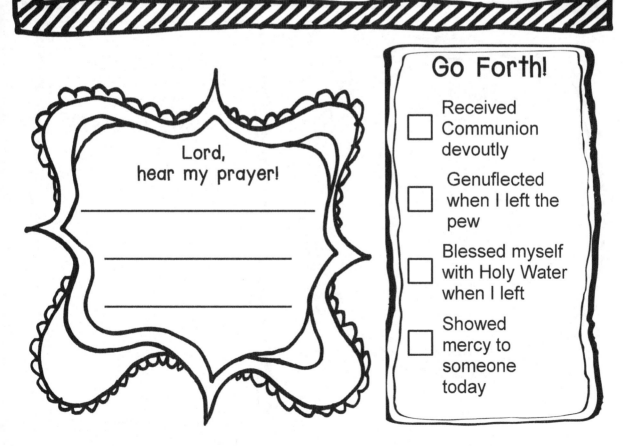

Lord,
hear my prayer!

_____

_____

_____

## Go Forth!

☐ Received Communion devoutly

☐ Genuflected when I left the pew

☐ Blessed myself with Holy Water when I left

☐ Showed mercy to someone today

# Am I Ready to Meet Jesus in the Mass?

## A CHECKLIST

☐ Morning Offering

☐ Had a good attitude when getting ready

☐ Fasted for 1 hour

☐ Arrived on Time

☐ Blessed myself with Holy Water

☐ Prayed before Mass Began

Liturgical Color

Make a tally mark each time you hear the words:
**"Jesus Christ"**

Responsorial Psalm

Gospel Story

Draw the Gospel Story

# Words to Listen For During Mass
## Circle each word you hear.

| | | |
|---|---|---|
| Apostles | Grace | Saint |
| Blessed Mother | Holy Spirit | Scripture |
| Communion | Mercy | Sin |
| Eucharist | Prayer | Trinity |
| Faith | Reconciliation | Trust |
| Forgiveness | Sacrament | Virtue |

Lord,
hear my prayer!

_____

_____

_____

## Go Forth!

☐ Received Communion devoutly

☐ Genuflected when I left the pew

☐ Blessed myself with Holy Water when I left

☐ Showed mercy to someone today

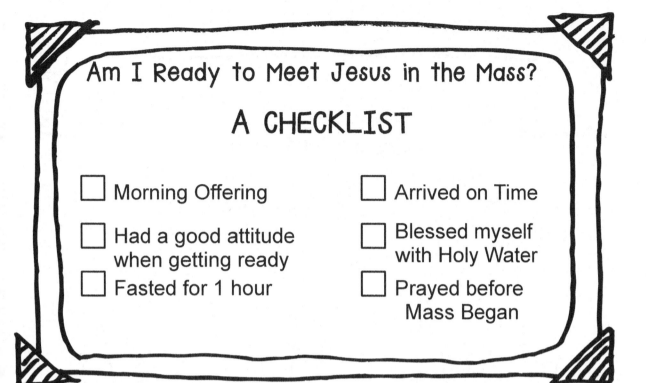

# Am I Ready to Meet Jesus in the Mass?

## A CHECKLIST

☐ Morning Offering

☐ Had a good attitude when getting ready

☐ Fasted for 1 hour

☐ Arrived on Time

☐ Blessed myself with Holy Water

☐ Prayed before Mass Began

Liturgical Color

Make a tally mark each time you hear the words:

**"Jesus Christ"**

Responsorial Psalm

Gospel Story

Draw the Gospel Story

# Words to Listen For During Mass
## Circle each word you hear.

| | | |
|---|---|---|
| Apostles | Grace | Saint |
| Blessed Mother | Holy Spirit | Scripture |
| Communion | Mercy | Sin |
| Eucharist | Prayer | Trinity |
| Faith | Reconciliation | Trust |
| Forgiveness | Sacrament | Virtue |

Lord,
hear my prayer!

_____

_____

_____

## Go Forth!

☐ Received Communion devoutly

☐ Genuflected when I left the pew

☐ Blessed myself with Holy Water when I left

☐ Showed mercy to someone today

## Am I Ready to Meet Jesus in the Mass?

## A CHECKLIST

☐ Morning Offering

☐ Had a good attitude when getting ready

☐ Fasted for 1 hour

☐ Arrived on Time

☐ Blessed myself with Holy Water

☐ Prayed before Mass Began

Liturgical Color

Make a tally mark each time you hear the words:
**"Jesus Christ"**

Responsorial Psalm

Gospel Story

Draw the Gospel Story

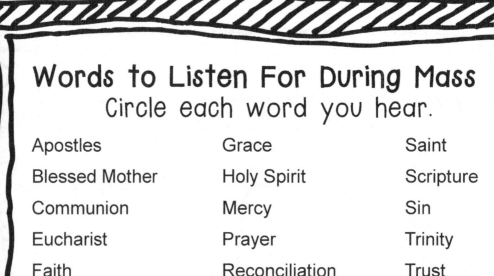

# Words to Listen For During Mass
## Circle each word you hear.

| | | |
|---|---|---|
| Apostles | Grace | Saint |
| Blessed Mother | Holy Spirit | Scripture |
| Communion | Mercy | Sin |
| Eucharist | Prayer | Trinity |
| Faith | Reconciliation | Trust |
| Forgiveness | Sacrament | Virtue |

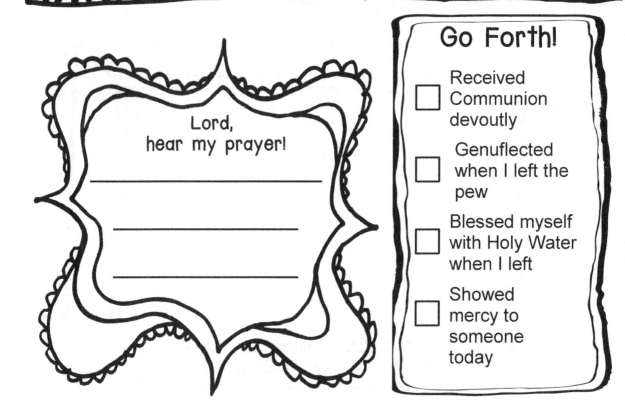

Lord,
hear my prayer!

_____

_____

_____

## Go Forth!

☐ Received Communion devoutly

☐ Genuflected when I left the pew

☐ Blessed myself with Holy Water when I left

☐ Showed mercy to someone today

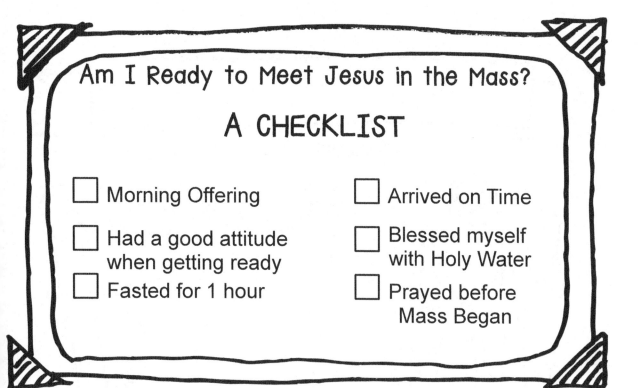

# Am I Ready to Meet Jesus in the Mass?

## A CHECKLIST

☐ Morning Offering

☐ Had a good attitude when getting ready

☐ Fasted for 1 hour

☐ Arrived on Time

☐ Blessed myself with Holy Water

☐ Prayed before Mass Began

Liturgical Color

Make a tally mark each time you hear the words:
## "Jesus Christ"

Responsorial Psalm

Gospel Story

Draw the Gospel Story

# Words to Listen For During Mass
## Circle each word you hear.

| | | |
|---|---|---|
| Apostles | Grace | Saint |
| Blessed Mother | Holy Spirit | Scripture |
| Communion | Mercy | Sin |
| Eucharist | Prayer | Trinity |
| Faith | Reconciliation | Trust |
| Forgiveness | Sacrament | Virtue |

Lord,
hear my prayer!

_____

_____

## Go Forth!

☐ Received Communion devoutly

☐ Genuflected when I left the pew

☐ Blessed myself with Holy Water when I left

☐ Showed mercy to someone today

## Am I Ready to Meet Jesus in the Mass?

## A CHECKLIST

☐ Morning Offering

☐ Had a good attitude when getting ready

☐ Fasted for 1 hour

☐ Arrived on Time

☐ Blessed myself with Holy Water

☐ Prayed before Mass Began

Liturgical Color

Make a tally mark each time you hear the words:
**"Jesus Christ"**

Responsorial Psalm

Gospel Story

Draw the Gospel Story

# Words to Listen For During Mass
## Circle each word you hear.

| | | |
|---|---|---|
| Apostles | Grace | Saint |
| Blessed Mother | Holy Spirit | Scripture |
| Communion | Mercy | Sin |
| Eucharist | Prayer | Trinity |
| Faith | Reconciliation | Trust |
| Forgiveness | Sacrament | Virtue |

Lord,
hear my prayer!

_____

_____

_____

## Go Forth!

☐ Received Communion devoutly

☐ Genuflected when I left the pew

☐ Blessed myself with Holy Water when I left

☐ Showed mercy to someone today

# Am I Ready to Meet Jesus in the Mass?

## A CHECKLIST

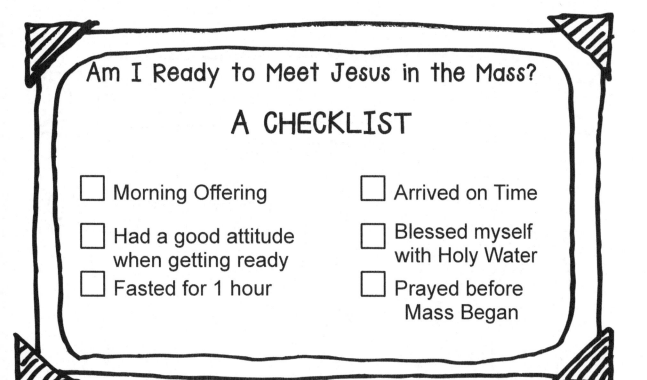

☐ Morning Offering

☐ Had a good attitude when getting ready

☐ Fasted for 1 hour

☐ Arrived on Time

☐ Blessed myself with Holy Water

☐ Prayed before Mass Began

Liturgical Color

Make a tally mark each time you hear the words:
**"Jesus Christ"**

Responsorial Psalm

Gospel Story

Draw the Gospel Story

# Words to Listen For During Mass
## Circle each word you hear.

| | | |
|---|---|---|
| Apostles | Grace | Saint |
| Blessed Mother | Holy Spirit | Scripture |
| Communion | Mercy | Sin |
| Eucharist | Prayer | Trinity |
| Faith | Reconciliation | Trust |
| Forgiveness | Sacrament | Virtue |

Lord,
hear my prayer!

_____

_____

_____

## Go Forth!

☐ Received Communion devoutly

☐ Genuflected when I left the pew

☐ Blessed myself with Holy Water when I left

☐ Showed mercy to someone today

# Am I Ready to Meet Jesus in the Mass?

## A CHECKLIST

☐ Morning Offering

☐ Had a good attitude when getting ready

☐ Fasted for 1 hour

☐ Arrived on Time

☐ Blessed myself with Holy Water

☐ Prayed before Mass Began

Liturgical Color

Make a tally mark each time you hear the words:
**"Jesus Christ"**

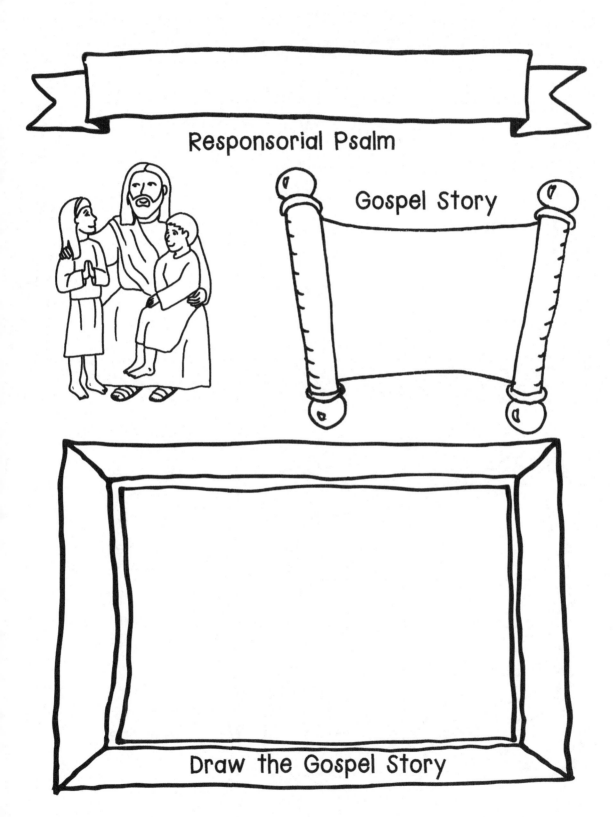

Responsorial Psalm

Gospel Story

Draw the Gospel Story

# Words to Listen For During Mass
## Circle each word you hear.

| | | |
|---|---|---|
| Apostles | Grace | Saint |
| Blessed Mother | Holy Spirit | Scripture |
| Communion | Mercy | Sin |
| Eucharist | Prayer | Trinity |
| Faith | Reconciliation | Trust |
| Forgiveness | Sacrament | Virtue |

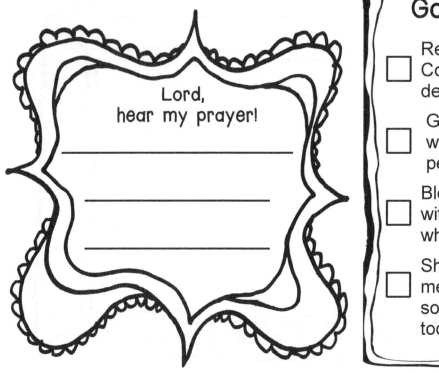

Lord,
hear my prayer!

_____

_____

_____

## Go Forth!

☐ Received Communion devoutly

☐ Genuflected when I left the pew

☐ Blessed myself with Holy Water when I left

☐ Showed mercy to someone today

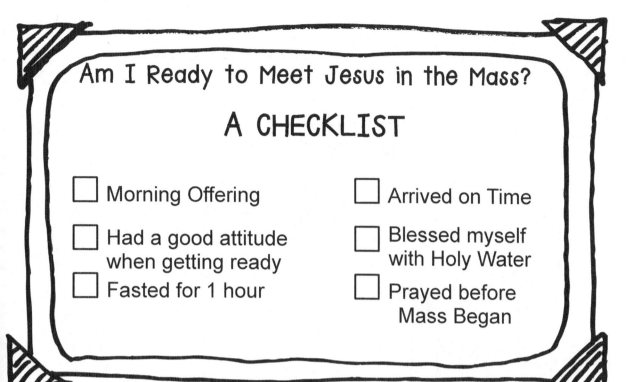

# Am I Ready to Meet Jesus in the Mass?

## A CHECKLIST

- ☐ Morning Offering
- ☐ Had a good attitude when getting ready
- ☐ Fasted for 1 hour

- ☐ Arrived on Time
- ☐ Blessed myself with Holy Water
- ☐ Prayed before Mass Began

Liturgical Color

Make a tally mark each time you hear the words:
**"Jesus Christ"**

Responsorial Psalm

Gospel Story

Draw the Gospel Story

# Words to Listen For During Mass
## Circle each word you hear.

| | | |
|---|---|---|
| Apostles | Grace | Saint |
| Blessed Mother | Holy Spirit | Scripture |
| Communion | Mercy | Sin |
| Eucharist | Prayer | Trinity |
| Faith | Reconciliation | Trust |
| Forgiveness | Sacrament | Virtue |

Lord,
hear my prayer!

_____

_____

_____

## Go Forth!

- ☐ Received Communion devoutly
- ☐ Genuflected when I left the pew
- ☐ Blessed myself with Holy Water when I left
- ☐ Showed mercy to someone today

# Am I Ready to Meet Jesus in the Mass?

## A CHECKLIST

☐ Morning Offering

☐ Had a good attitude when getting ready

☐ Fasted for 1 hour

☐ Arrived on Time

☐ Blessed myself with Holy Water

☐ Prayed before Mass Began

Liturgical Color

Make a tally mark each time you hear the words:
**"Jesus Christ"**

Responsorial Psalm

Gospel Story

Draw the Gospel Story

# Words to Listen For During Mass
## Circle each word you hear.

| | | |
|---|---|---|
| Apostles | Grace | Saint |
| Blessed Mother | Holy Spirit | Scripture |
| Communion | Mercy | Sin |
| Eucharist | Prayer | Trinity |
| Faith | Reconciliation | Trust |
| Forgiveness | Sacrament | Virtue |

Lord,
hear my prayer!

_____

_____

_____

## Go Forth!

☐ Received Communion devoutly

☐ Genuflected when I left the pew

☐ Blessed myself with Holy Water when I left

☐ Showed mercy to someone today

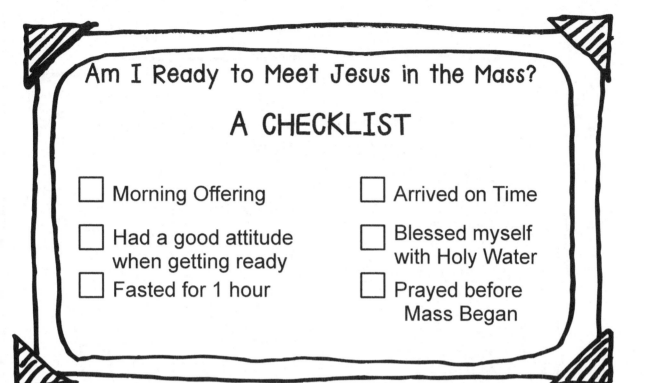

## Am I Ready to Meet Jesus in the Mass?

## A CHECKLIST

- ☐ Morning Offering
- ☐ Had a good attitude when getting ready
- ☐ Fasted for 1 hour
- ☐ Arrived on Time
- ☐ Blessed myself with Holy Water
- ☐ Prayed before Mass Began

Liturgical Color

Make a tally mark each time you hear the words:
**"Jesus Christ"**

Responsorial Psalm

Gospel Story

Draw the Gospel Story

# Words to Listen For During Mass
## Circle each word you hear.

| | | |
|---|---|---|
| Apostles | Grace | Saint |
| Blessed Mother | Holy Spirit | Scripture |
| Communion | Mercy | Sin |
| Eucharist | Prayer | Trinity |
| Faith | Reconciliation | Trust |
| Forgiveness | Sacrament | Virtue |

Lord,
hear my prayer!

_____

_____

_____

## Go Forth!

☐ Received Communion devoutly

☐ Genuflected when I left the pew

☐ Blessed myself with Holy Water when I left

☐ Showed mercy to someone today

# Am I Ready to Meet Jesus in the Mass?

## A CHECKLIST

☐ Morning Offering

☐ Had a good attitude when getting ready

☐ Fasted for 1 hour

☐ Arrived on Time

☐ Blessed myself with Holy Water

☐ Prayed before Mass Began

Liturgical Color

Make a tally mark each time you hear the words:
**"Jesus Christ"**

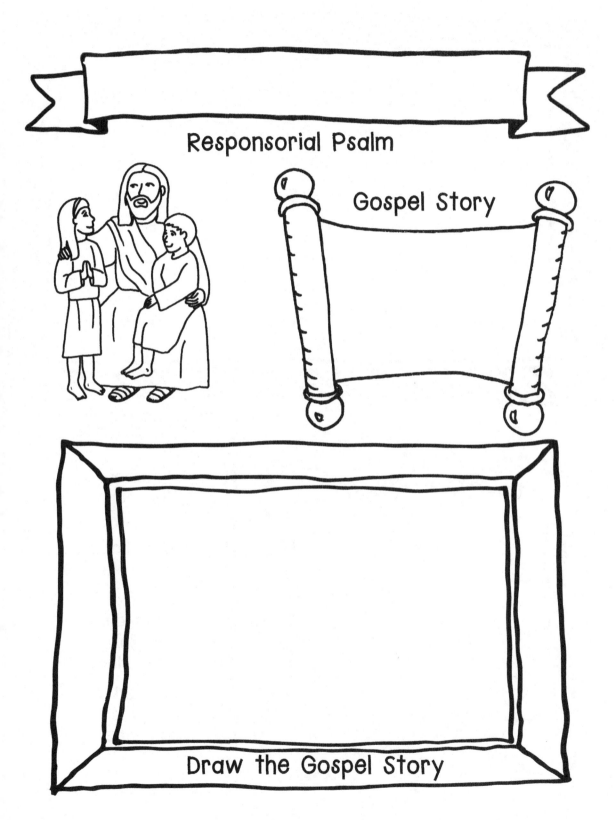

Responsorial Psalm

Gospel Story

Draw the Gospel Story

# Words to Listen For During Mass
## Circle each word you hear.

| | | |
|---|---|---|
| Apostles | Grace | Saint |
| Blessed Mother | Holy Spirit | Scripture |
| Communion | Mercy | Sin |
| Eucharist | Prayer | Trinity |
| Faith | Reconciliation | Trust |
| Forgiveness | Sacrament | Virtue |

Lord,
hear my prayer!

_____

_____

_____

## Go Forth!

☐ Received Communion devoutly

☐ Genuflected when I left the pew

☐ Blessed myself with Holy Water when I left

☐ Showed mercy to someone today

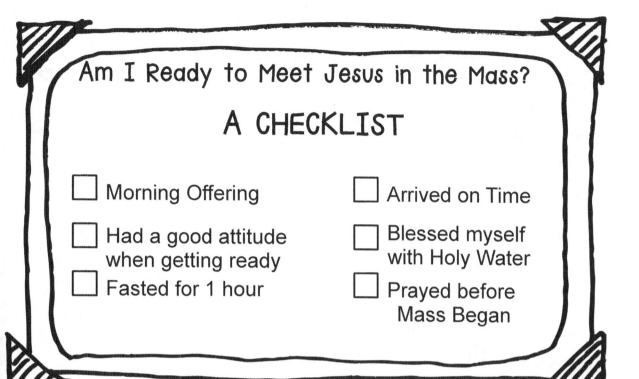

# Am I Ready to Meet Jesus in the Mass?

## A CHECKLIST

☐ Morning Offering

☐ Had a good attitude when getting ready

☐ Fasted for 1 hour

☐ Arrived on Time

☐ Blessed myself with Holy Water

☐ Prayed before Mass Began

Liturgical Color

Make a tally mark each time you hear the words:
**"Jesus Christ"**

Responsorial Psalm

Gospel Story

Draw the Gospel Story

# Words to Listen For During Mass
## Circle each word you hear.

| | | |
|---|---|---|
| Apostles | Grace | Saint |
| Blessed Mother | Holy Spirit | Scripture |
| Communion | Mercy | Sin |
| Eucharist | Prayer | Trinity |
| Faith | Prayer | Trust |
| Forgiveness | Reconciliation | Trust |
| Forgiveness | Sacrament | Virtue |

Lord,
hear my prayer!

_____

_____

_____

## Go Forth!

☐ Received Communion devoutly

☐ Genuflected when I left the pew

☐ Blessed myself with Holy Water when I left

☐ Showed mercy to someone today

# Am I Ready to Meet Jesus in the Mass?

## A CHECKLIST

☐ Morning Offering

☐ Had a good attitude when getting ready

☐ Fasted for 1 hour

☐ Arrived on Time

☐ Blessed myself with Holy Water

☐ Prayed before Mass Began

Liturgical Color

Make a tally mark each time you hear the words: **"Jesus Christ"**

Responsorial Psalm

Gospel Story

Draw the Gospel Story

# Words to Listen For During Mass
## Circle each word you hear.

| | | |
|---|---|---|
| Apostles | Grace | Saint |
| Blessed Mother | Holy Spirit | Scripture |
| Communion | Mercy | Sin |
| Eucharist | Prayer | Trinity |
| Faith | Reconciliation | Trust |
| Forgiveness | Sacrament | Virtue |

Lord,
hear my prayer!

_____

_____

_____

## Go Forth!

☐ Received Communion devoutly

☐ Genuflected when I left the pew

☐ Blessed myself with Holy Water when I left

☐ Showed mercy to someone today

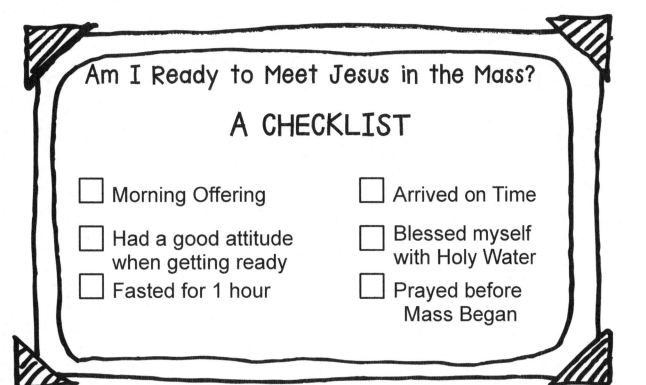

# Am I Ready to Meet Jesus in the Mass?

## A CHECKLIST

- ☐ Morning Offering
- ☐ Had a good attitude when getting ready
- ☐ Fasted for 1 hour

- ☐ Arrived on Time
- ☐ Blessed myself with Holy Water
- ☐ Prayed before Mass Began

Liturgical Color

Make a tally mark each time you hear the words:
**"Jesus Christ"**

Responsorial Psalm

Gospel Story

Draw the Gospel Story

# Words to Listen For During Mass
## Circle each word you hear.

| | | |
|---|---|---|
| Apostles | Grace | Saint |
| Blessed Mother | Holy Spirit | Scripture |
| Communion | Mercy | Sin |
| Eucharist | Prayer | Trinity |
| Faith | Reconciliation | Trust |
| Forgiveness | Sacrament | Virtue |

Lord,
hear my prayer!

_____

_____

_____

## Go Forth!

☐ Received Communion devoutly

☐ Genuflected when I left the pew

☐ Blessed myself with Holy Water when I left

☐ Showed mercy to someone today

# Am I Ready to Meet Jesus in the Mass?

## A CHECKLIST

- ☐ Morning Offering
- ☐ Had a good attitude when getting ready
- ☐ Fasted for 1 hour

- ☐ Arrived on Time
- ☐ Blessed myself with Holy Water
- ☐ Prayed before Mass Began

Liturgical Color

Make a tally mark each time you hear the words:
**"Jesus Christ"**

Responsorial Psalm

Gospel Story

Draw the Gospel Story

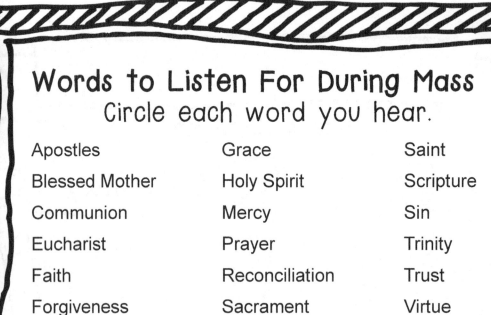

# Words to Listen For During Mass
## Circle each word you hear.

| | | |
|---|---|---|
| Apostles | Grace | Saint |
| Blessed Mother | Holy Spirit | Scripture |
| Communion | Mercy | Sin |
| Eucharist | Prayer | Trinity |
| Faith | Reconciliation | Trust |
| Forgiveness | Sacrament | Virtue |

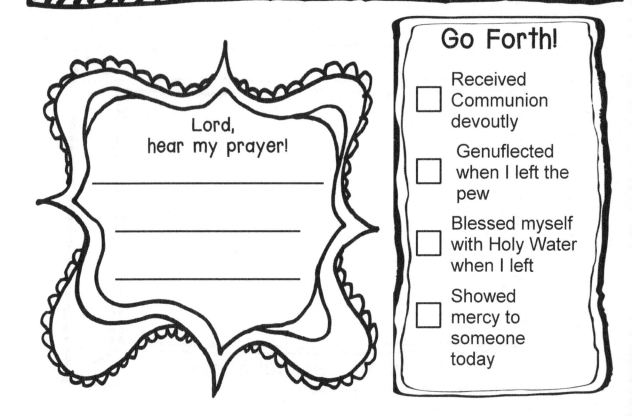

Lord,
hear my prayer!

_____

_____

_____

## Go Forth!

- ☐ Received Communion devoutly
- ☐ Genuflected when I left the pew
- ☐ Blessed myself with Holy Water when I left
- ☐ Showed mercy to someone today

# RECONCILIATION RECORD

Name: _____

Dates:

1. ———————        7. ———————

2. ———————        8. ———————

3. ———————        9. ———————

4. ———————        10. ———————

5. ———————        11. ———————

6. ———————        12. ———————

Made in the USA
Middletown, DE
07 October 2020